GERTRUDE STEIN
GERTRUDE STEIN
GERTRUDE STEIN

Random House   New York

GERTRUDE STEIN GERTRUDE STEIN GERTRUDE STEIN

A One-Character Play
by
Marty Martin

As Commissioned by Pat Carroll

Library of Congress Cataloging in Publication Data

Martin, Marty.
Gertrude Stein Gertrude Stein Gertrude Stein.

1. Stein, Gertrude, 1874–1946, in fiction, drama, poetry,
etc. I. Title.
[PS3563.A726G4   1980b]   812'.54   80–15197
ISBN 0–394–51199–9

Manufactured in the United States of America
23456789
First Edition

*For Pat Carroll
and 3504 Sirius*

GERTRUDE STEIN GERTRUDE STEIN GERTRUDE STEIN *was first presented by Sea-Ker, Inc., Mary Ellyn Devery, Producer, at the Circle Repertory Company, New York City, June 6, 1979, starring Pat Carroll as Gertrude Stein. Later, on October 23, 1979, the play moved to the Provincetown Playhouse, New York City.*

Directed by:
Milton Moss

Set by:
Anne Gibson

Lighting by:
Ruth Roberts

Costume by:
Garland Riddle

Introduction

In all of the voluminous literature that has been written about Gertrude Stein, there is very little that gives us any clue as to what she was like in person. The preponderance of exegesis on her work, while in the main useful and helpful, has been pretty much one-sided. This unfortunate imbalance has been amply corrected by Marty Martin's *Gertrude Stein Gertrude Stein Gertrude Stein*, as anyone who has been fortunate enough to see Pat Carroll in it can testify. It is an extraordinary work of art on many levels. It brings Stein to life so vividly that for many people the image of the real Gertrude has begun to fuse with that of Pat Carroll. So lifelike is it that some persons who actually knew Stein have wept unabashedly and uncontrollably on seeing this play. But perhaps more astounding than this *verismo* effect is the success that the play achieves in what is probably the most difficult of all theatrical genres, the monologue. Here we have a play with no action. Carroll—Gertrude Stein—occasionally rises from her chair to consult a dictionary or to turn on a light, but essentially it is a static play. It deals almost exclusively with thoughts and emotions. At first, it appears to be a one-character play—but do not be fooled. It is most definitely a two-character play. And by this I do not mean to refer to the off-stage presence of Alice B. Toklas (the B is for "Babette," Stein informs us). It is, rather, the audience that becomes, must become, the other character. Sometimes it takes the audience a little while to realize that it must do more than merely sit back and be amused.

We *are* amused, of course, but to get the full enjoyment of the play we must participate—we must play back to Stein. And when this happens, as it usually does, the fun heightens and the intensity of the play reaches such proportions that audiences invariably rise to their feet for a standing ovation at the play's conclusion.

When any unusual work of art makes its appearance, there is, inevitably, a pocket of resistance to it by persons, perhaps well-meaning but alas, not sufficiently open-minded to perceive the miracle that has occurred. This happened back in 1933 when Stein herself published *The Autobiography of Alice B. Toklas*—and almost at once Matisse and several other painters and writers (who should have known better) issued a printed protest against her supposed inaccuracies, not realizing that she had created a literary masterpiece, not a factual documentation of an era. Every artist knows that he must select, rearrange, perhaps even distort the raw material to make the creation what it is—a work of art. Therefore, I should like to add a cautionary word here to readers of this play. Do *not* approach it as though it were the Gospel According to Saint Gertrude. There are omissions, there is considerable telescoping of time and events, and perhaps even an occasional factual inaccuracy. But this is all deliberate, in order to create a total impression. The purpose of this play is not to instruct—that is the function of textbooks. It is to bring us the exquisite pleasure of getting to know Gertrude Stein herself. So, in coming to this play, let us do what Stein tells us her professor at Radcliffe, William James, advised her to do—i.e., keep a window in the attic of your mind open. Not cracked, but open. With such an open mind, this can be a magical experience, as, indeed, Stein's whole *oeuvre* can be.

From the very start of this work we are taken into Stein's confidence. Nothing is withheld. She shares with us her joys and sorrows, her dislikes and her enthusiasms, but above all, her gusto and zest for life, communicated through mere words—words that were her lifelong passion and concern. But we are presented with a great deal more than the physical presence and personality of Gertrude Stein in this play. The words of the playwright, while in part derived, of course, from Stein's own writings, are so skillfully wrought that we get the immediate impression of meeting the characters who do not actually appear physically on stage—and what characters they are, starting with Alice B. Toklas and including Ernest Hemingway, Sherwood Anderson, Scott and Zelda Fitzgerald, Marie Laurencin, Guillaume Apollinaire, Sylvia Beach, Rousseau, and Pablo Picasso, among a host of others. In short, we get to know the entire group of expatriates who centered in Paris in the now-legendary twenties, along with the painters who became the giants of modern art. We are given the privilege of meeting the movers and shakers of twentieth-century culture.

Perhaps the high point of the show—if, indeed, any one portion can be singled out as being more memorable than another—is Stein's recounting of the Banquet Rousseau, a party arranged by Picasso and his mistress, Fernande Olivier, in honor of the gentle, elderly painter of primitive pictures, the Douanier Rousseau. Surely this must have been the most bizarre party ever held. But this entire play is a banquet. So come, partake, be greedy. Come back and refill your plate as often as you wish. There's enough to go around for as many helpings as you want. The supply never runs out. Enjoy.

Robert A. Wilson

GERTRUDE STEIN
GERTRUDE STEIN
GERTRUDE STEIN

ACT ONE

Incidental music incidentally. Incidental music and incidentally. Incidental and incidental incidental music and and incidentally. Alright then. Lights. The studio at 27 rue de Fleurus in Paris 1938. Heavy wooden furniture, particularly the high-backed thronelike Renaissance armchair and the long table strewn with artifacts and piles of books counterbalanced at one end by a single huge Webster's dictionary. China pieces of questionable good taste adorn the mantle and the walls are covered up to the high ceiling with modern oil paintings on canvas. Some are framed and some are not. Rainfall and a gentle rumble of distant thunder. And GERTRUDE STEIN. Simultaneously. She is wearing her long brown corduroy robe is sitting in her armchair quietly smoking a cigarette and pondering aloud incidentally. There is the sound of rain and distant thunder.

It is   it always is   and it always most certainly is
an inconvenience being evicted   I know   and we
were. Alice did not like it   Alice Toklas   and she
said so   she said   who are you to be telling us
our home today is to be someone else's home tomorrow   and he said I am the landlord Madame   that
is who I am   and he was   and he is   and we are
evicted   and that as they say is that. And the landlord's son moves in tomorrow.   Well anyway.

Before I came to be living here   I was going to be
not being living there   there is in America   of
course it naturally is   and I wanted to be going
away   not to be coming back until I was a lion   a
real lion. Sometimes only in exile can one truly repre-
sent one's country   that was true of Dante and it is
true of me   which reminds me of eviction and packing   I do not want to be reminded of packing   I
hate packing   so I will be reminded of something
else   immediately Picasso comes to mind.

But before I am reminded of Picasso   I must be reminded of Alice Toklas   who is at the present mo-
ment sound asleep in her room. Alice asked me to wake
her in three hours if it stops raining she said. Well it
has now been six hours and it is still raining   I do
not know what to do.

Well. Alice knows not to trust me with a task. Tasks
are things I cannot do   they make me nervous. I

can drive a car and walk around and talk simply and straightforwardly and I can write   of course   and read and eat food   but anything beyond that makes me nervous.   The most difficult part about being a genius is you have to sit around all the time doing absolutely nothing   you just do. Alice. But she will want to be packing things   oh dear and that reminds me of moving   and that reminds me of eviction and landlords and expired leases   oh dear   I would rather be reminded of the day I moved in   it is more pleasant   yes   much more. Leo was there of course   Leo Stein   my brother who is two years older than I   it was originally his *pavillon*   by that I mean he found it and lived here alone for a time   and then I came to twenty-seven rue de Fleurus   and then all who followed after that   but that will all come later.

Leo was at that time an art enthusiast   a quattrocento art enthusiast   quattrocento art being his forte   and the subject of his studies   and the object of his fleeting passions   how he loved the Italian.

Anyway   one was immediately impressed upon entering his *pavillon* with Leo Stein's good taste in art prints   especially Japanese landscapes   every wall was covered with Japanese landscapes   when I first arrived   I remember thinking   how odd to be a quattrocento art enthusiast living in a Japanese landscape in Paris   yet how very odd   and it was   and that is the first thing I thought when I arrived at my brother's *pavillon*.

We had grown up in California together   he and I   and at that time our tastes were much the same   but I did not like that specializing in quattrocento art so

much   although some of the Japanese prints were
interesting   and I had just arrived and everything
was beginning to be beginning for me   and Leo and
I were glad to be being in one another's company
again. It is always best being the youngest in the family   I was   and it is best   it just is   everyone
watches out for you   and it saves you a lot of
bother   of course   when you grow up then you
remain a child and that is both good and bad. For
those who appreciate me   like Sylvia Beach   I remain the infant prodigy   but as far as Wyndham
Lewis is concerned   I am a huge dogmatic child   so
you see   it is both good and bad. Anyway that is the
way it was   and Leo looked after me when I first
arrived and it was all very interesting.

The weather was nice   and we walked everywhere immediately. Paris had not changed consid-
erably   since I was three   it still smelled of leather
and perfume and that was nice.   Leo was troubled
because he had reached a dead end with Leonardo
de Vinci   trying to comprehend his mind   and we
touched on genius   but nothing really got said   except that another enthusiasm seemed to be taking the
place of his already famous one for quattrocento
art   and that was actually painting   with paint. He
had already talked himself out of devoting his intellectual life to the pursuits of biology, esthetics,
philosophy and history   and now   evidently   it
was to be so with quattrocento art and did   I think
so. Well.

I said   anything is a walk   a stroll in the park
is a walk but this is a conversation   and so I
said   you have a habit of draining out your energies
in analysis and conversation   and he did   and he

did not like that   not at all   and so we talked about other things and walked everywhere immediately and he told me about his talks with Pablo Casals and how they discussed art weekly over dinner   which had made him want to try his own hand at painting   Leo   and so he rushed home   and built a fire in the stove   took off all his clothes and began making sketches from the nude   although he never said what Casals did that night   I suppose he played his cello.

Later we met his friends the Berensons   Bernard and his wife   and we dined   and they played a game where someone chose a photograph of a painting   and then they covered it with a tablecloth   that had a small hole in it   and once they had done this they would proceed to try and guess from some small detail of the painting who the artist was. Berenson was an authority   but Leo often guessed correctly   especially if the artist was a quattrocento one. I seldom ever knew but I laughed a lot.

In fact   it was while playing that game one night that Bernard Berenson said to Leo   perhaps if you cannot be a great painter   you will be a great collector then   and Leo agreed   and the next day we combed the galleries and shops of Paris looking for something new   but we were disappointed   and Bernard said   have you ever heard of Cézanne   and we said we had not   where does one find him   and he said   at Vollard's   Vollard's on the rue LaFitte   and so the next day we went to Ambroise Vollard's tiny little shop on the rue LaFitte. In the doorway of the tiny shop was a huge dark man peering ominously into the street. That was Vollard   cheerful

He was himself a collector *extraordinaire*   Vol- lard   he had been so always   when he was little he collected rocks from his mother's garden   it pleased him greatly then and it pleased him greatly now to be collecting the first pieces of art that separated the twentieth century from the nineteenth century and which utterly shocked Paris in those days   although I must confess I did not take to them immedi- ately   though Leo   Leo did Leo did   Leo did. But first.

Entering the shop was a thing unto itself   once we had crossed the threshold   Leo and I found ourselves in a store that could easily have been mistaken for a junk shop   everything was covered by at least one layer of dust   and for a minute we were afraid to move lest we disturb some structure that had been in progress for centuries   but anyway   Leo finally said something   the Cézannes   we want to see the Cézannes   Ah said Vollard   and he disappeared upstairs.

My brother and I waited anxiously   but he was gone a long time   and he was gone a longer time   and then we heard footsteps   and he returned with a painting of an apple and we said no.

Then he disappeared again   and Leo called after him   a landscape   and when Vollard returned he was carrying a painting of a nude   but it was a Cé- zanne   at that time   we were not yet ready for Cézanne nudes   and so I said   yes   but we want a landscape   a sunny one   and Leo said   prefer- ably not unfinished   and Vollard mumbled some- thing under his breath and disappeared again. It grew dark outside and we waited   and then we heard the

Vollard appears at top right: 9

footsteps but this time it was an old charwoman who emerged from the stairway   and she looked at us   and then she quietly walked out the door   and then more footsteps down the stairs and another old charwoman emerged and she did the same thing   and I said   the truth is   there really is no Cézanne these old women do it all in the attic.

Then   Vollard   reappeared.   He   was   carrying   a landscape   this   time   a   green   Cézanne   land-scape   green   green   and we liked it   we both did   and we conferred and then we bought it. Little did we realize at the time that we had just taken the first step toward planting ourselves in the center of an art movement the likes of which the outside world had never known.

Now that is what they call the art of building sus-pense.   And I really ought to go wake Alice up now   I really should   but she so dislikes a rainy day   it makes her melancholy   she is like that   and I am not. Sometimes it is nice just to sit and listen to the rain and make the past the present   that is what art is   making the past the present   and making the present a continuous one.

A portrait of the autumn exhibition in Paris when I was twenty-nine by Gertrude   Gertrude Stein. A building   a line up to the door   a crowd around the painting inside. And. Whispers.

Not-without-malice-whispers.

What is it   what is what   what is that   what is that   A painting of a lady with a hat   with a hat.

Oh.   What is that line of green on her nose   on
her nose   on her nose green was seen   I suppose   I suppose   Really do you think so.

Never mind.

And another one said   nastiest smear of paint I ever
laid my eyes on

Really do you think so.

I thought I told you.

What a fine gathering.   And someone else said who
is responsible for this outrage   to which Matisse re-
plied   I am   and then he left. One can hardly
blame him   it was a portrait of his wife. Leo did not
like the painting either   naturally of course   I did
and so we bought it.

Well the new Matisse   looked lovely beside the green
Cézanne landscape   and the Cézanne nudes   they
were inevitable   although it did   the Matisse   make
a little argument when placed next to the black and
white by Manet   and we knew better than to group it
with the two Renoirs   they were so small   it would
have eaten them up   completely   entirely   but
all in all the art wall was beginning to be a beginning   and even after we added a pair of medium-
sized Gauguins   it was the lady with the hat   the
Matisse who remained the jewel that stood out among
the rest.

Leo was pleased with himself and he was pleased with
the world at large   just knowing that one did not

have to be a millionaire to own an oil   as for me   I was pleased because it was by the light of those paintings that I first began to write   but first.

It is often true in the twenty-ninth year of one's life   when one is twenty-nine   that all the wild energies that are thrown off by the creative process of the making of a personality begin to take form and shape   this one may be pointed like an arrow   that one branched out like that   and this one may be circular   but it is often true in the twenty-ninth year   whether really or metaphorically   that these energies begin to assume a decided shape   and one is confronted with the question of one's purpose   and life which was all a blurry splash of color narrows down to an acutely focused arrangement of patterns. I wonder if that was clear. Oh well   no doubt I will continue doing it. And so in that twenty-ninth year   one is usually forced or obliged or inspired to make a choice about one's inner life and whether to acknowledge and express or obscure as best as possible that inner life. Now then. When Leo and I were growing up together in California and our family being the way it was   none of us knew anything of one another's inner lives   not anything. But it is that inner life   it is that one   it is that thing   that is the actual life of any individual   and none of us knew anything about each other's actual lives   because no one in the family had the vision it takes to see an inner life   much less the skillful audacity required to share one   and we talked about it later   Leo and I   when we were in Paris   but we never talked about it then   we were too young   and our inner lives were kept secret   although   later   years later   when Leo underwent psychoanalysis   he blamed this necessity to keep his inner life secret on

the American middle-class habit of discouraging self-
expression. Well Leo thought a lot but I tend to dis-
agree. I think it was because our parents were a
bore   a real bore.

They had planned on five children   and they had
planned their little lives for them in advance of their
birth but the two youngest ones died in their infancy
and were immediately replaced by Leo and me   in
that order. It was a queer thing to think about being
born under such circumstances   it makes one feel
funny   it just does   and so we rarely thought
about it   Leo and I   but when we did it made us
wonder about purpose behind life   and so by my
twenty-ninth year   haunted all the while by that
fact   I finally decided to devote myself to writing.
Leo was immediately skeptical   no doubt it stemmed
from envy because he had not yet reached the twenty-
ninth year of his life and he was already well into his
thirties.

But whether or not he had a theme   Leo   he had
a definite flair for explaining things   and he had a
definite need to be explaining them   and so by and
by as people began coming to the rue de Fleurus to
see the Matisses and the Cézannes and the Gauguins   he would explain to them whatever he felt
needed explaining at the time   which was usually his
expert if not somewhat tortured analysis of modern
art   and so began the Saturday evenings at twenty-
seven rue de Fleurus.

It was of necessity that we became formal about
it   people were coming and going and coming back
again with more people. Some we knew some we
did   not know   and it was very interesting   but

14   it was becoming a nuisance   particularly because I
had just begun devoting myself to writing and I was
writing a book called *Three Lives* and I wanted to
achieve the same effect in literature as was achieved by
Cézanne and Matisse in their painting with regard to
total impression and the portrayal of character through
the use of unorthodox colors and textures and I wanted
to accomplish that and I wanted to accomplish it in
literature   to do with words what they did with
paint   to use a new metaphor in writing that was at
that time exclusive to painting and I did it   and I did
it by the light of their paintings and it worked and I
called it *Three Lives*. But it was not to be written with
people coming and going and at all hours   and so the
Saturday evenings evolved out of necessity and only
after nine o'clock. It was my habit then to begin writing at about eleven o'clock because I like eleven o'clock
and because there was rarely a knock on the door at
that hour   and so I would start around then and
write until dawn.

Sentences and words are a passion   and they do
not   just   happen   they evolve gradually and that
usually takes until dawn   then I would go to bed
and sleep until noon   to be awakened by the sound
of beating of rugs in the courtyard which was as dis-
agreeable as it was effective   but Helene the housekeeper had her own set of passions. For example   she
did not care for Matisse.   Her omelettes and soufflés
were her specialty   but for Matisse she always fried
the eggs. It requires the same amount of eggs and butter she said   but it lacks respect. Everybody is a
critic but Helene was an excellent housekeeper too
and she was with us until nineteen thirteen and then
she was not with us anymore   but as long as she

was she cleaned and cooked for us especially on
Saturday evenings when everybody came and brought
somebody.

The group usually arrived about nine o'clock and I
would greet them at the door and show them into the
studio where Leo was frequently to be found lying on
the floor with his feet propped up and supported by a
bookcase   it is good for the indigestion he would
say and an exotic cure was always a thing of joy for
Leo even if there was no exotic ailment for it to act
upon.

Isadora came and brought somebody   Isadora Duncan with the scarves   and if Leo loved the Italian   she
loved the Greek even more   anything that was below the Greek was below the Greek   Isadora was
like that. She and Raymond   Raymond was her
brother   she and Raymond Duncan grew up in San
Francisco too and now they lived down the street
from us on the rue de Fleurus   and they made these
sandals for me and they made a pair for Leo. They
had just returned from Greece the Duncans and now
they were Greek. They were not going to be Italian
renaissance anymore and even that was better than
their Omar Khayyám stage.

Well one night Isadora danced a little she always did
and Raymond looked at the paintings   and announced
that since he had become a Greek his taste in art was
now perfect and he found the paintings ugly. We
showed the Duncans out and did not ask them back
although years later we were saddened to learn that
Isadora Duncan-with-the-scarves had gotten one of
them caught in the spokes of the wheels of somebody's

convertible going forty-five miles an hour and died in-
stantly. Sad   but still affectations can be danger-
ous   as Leo pointed out pointed out pointed out.

He and not the paintings ultimately became the point
of interest and attraction at the Saturday evenings. It
was Leo's personality and presence which created the
reputation of the Stein salon at that time when many
of the artists and writers whom we had met at the
cafés came to take tea and to match intellects with Leo
on the subject of modern art while I sat in my armchair quietly listening   yes quietly. They often went
away laughing and mocking but all the same they
were changed by what they heard and saw.   Some
found him obnoxious   others charming   but whatever he was   he was impressive   Leo   and for
Paris then and for modern art   he was a vital
force   and when he was not expounding his theories
or improving his digestion   he was singing and dancing   and one lady told him his imitation of Isadora
Duncan was too sensitive to be satire and he thanked
her   he was not without his charm. She was also the
person who told me that I did not look ladylike while
smoking a cigar   and I thanked her too upon exhaling.

All in all everyone who came to see the pictures was
in one way or another impressed   especially with
Cézanne and Matisse   but the artist   the painting
that was to become the largest part of me and of my
life   was a portrait of myself   as yet unpainted by
a young and almost completely unknown artist   a
Spaniard   which does   which finally brings me to
the subject of Picasso   Pablo Picasso.

But first.

Genius is to me the rarest of human qualities   it is
the art of becoming legendary. I have always adored
legends   and I have always admired geniuses who
get themselves into them. And with art it is always a
funny thing   which is more important   the artist
or the art   well no matter which one you start with
it always leads to the other. Picasso was his paintings   and his paintings were Picasso and everyone
who knew him knew that.

Picasso was discovered by me according to me   and
he was discovered by Leo   according to Leo. Well
we argued and we finally decided that Leo could be
the discoverer of the works of Picasso in Paris if I
could be the discoverer of the man himself and that is
how history resolves a conflict and we were both
pleased then according to Picasso.   I wonder if Alice
is going to sleep forever.

He lived in a little place Picasso   that was called
the Bateau Lavoir   it was called that because it was
near the Seine and it looked like the laundry barges
that floated down it   and it was a double irony Bateau
Lavoir because the building only had one faucet. This
he shared with the poet Max Jacob and a very lively
person by the name of Fernande Olivier. I must go on
about Fernande a bit.

She was called *la belle* Fernande for her charm and
spirit. She had escaped from an early marriage and a
life in the provinces   into the extraordinary world
of the struggling artists and poets who lived in the
Latin Quarter in Paris then and she and Picasso tor-
mented each other lovingly for more than twelve
years. She saw him through his blue period and the
rose period and the harlequin period and she watched

his work absorbing the influence of the African art
that was his Spanish heritage gradually becoming more
and more geometrical   and free of the limitations of
realism and it excited her   she was no fool   but she
wore hats a lot and I have often found that women
who like to wear hats a lot are usually   well anyway.

Picasso now was a more intense individual   a quiet
one. Some thought him remote   but he was not nor
was he intimate   he was just totally there always. He
carried his head like a priceless bust   like a bull-
fighter   the shoulders held a certain way and his eyes
were dark   which is always dramatic   and they
drank up everything they saw. Leo said his gaze was
so absorbing   Picasso's   that whenever he looked
at a picture one was surprised to find anything left on
the paper afterwards.

Leo discovered the artist's work in a little café run
by Clovis Sagot   the retired clown   who showed
the Picassos he had to Leo and said this is the real
thing   and Leo bought one   an ugly one   and
then he took me back to the café with him to buy
another. Leo was particularly taken with a painting
by Picasso of a young girl with a basket of flowers
and the legs and feet of a monkey   I hated it. We
knew her   she had nice feet   she sold flowers
outside the Moulin Rouge   and to me it was not
her   the picture   and so we argued   Leo and
I   in front of Sagot until Sagot finally threatened
to guillotine the legs and so we left without the painting   arguing. Then at dinner the next night Leo
said that he had gone ahead and purchased it   and I
threw my napkin down   my appetite was ruined.

But if Picasso's paintings did not immediately captivate my interest   the man who painted them did. It was not long before he and Fernande showed up at the Stein salon to see the paintings   his hanging beside Renoirs and Gauguins and Cézannes and Matisses and they brought the gang with them   the poets and the painters from the Latin Quarter   many of whom had followed Picasso all the way from Barcelona. Yes   it really was a movement. And it was beginning to be getting big.

Now Max Jacob whom they brought with them was not just a poet he told fortunes and as they say   he was the life of every party and then Apollinaire started coming over. Guillaume Apollinaire was another friend of Picasso's and a poet too. He was of all the regulars who came then perhaps the most loved   but he had a funny way of doing this with his lips to give bite to what he said   you have such skinny fingers he would say to Marie Laurencin with his lips like that.

Marie Laurencin and Apollinaire were lovers then and in those days Fernande was *la belle* Fernande   Picasso was Pablo   I was Gertrude or Mademoiselle Zhertrude   Max was Max   and Apollinaire was Guillaume   but Marie Laurencin was always Marie Laurencin   she is still Marie Laurencin   Marie would not do   it is not enough   it has to be the whole thing always with her   and so she was always Marie Laurencin   and she still is.

She was a painter   Marie Laurencin   the only woman painter in the movement and very strange. She did a portrait of Picasso   Fernande   Apollinaire   and herself and it was very strange   and I bought it from her   she had never sold one before. Apollinaire was so pleased that he wrote a little pamphlet about the movement in which he referred to it as cubist   he was the first to call it that   and everybody then was pleased   especially Marie Laurencin   who was now being exhibited beside Picasso and Matisse.

Her first visit to the rue de Fleurus was an event   a real one   it was not on a Saturday nor was it before eleven   but she was so interesting and so we let her in   what the hell. The first thing she did was to fall   she was terribly near-sighted and things got in her way a lot   she did not wear eyeglasses   the French people never do   she always used a lorgnette   and the next thing she did was to examine every picture within reach going over them one inch at a time with the lorgnette.

I prefer portraits   she finally said   being one myself   I am a Clouet   you know   and she was a perfect Clouet. We sat down together and she told me her life history   and of how in all the years that she and Guillaume had been lovers   her mother   with whom she lived alone   had never known. She did not care much for men   her mother   and their apartment was rather like a convent but then the mother died and it did not seem to matter to Marie Laurencin anymore   and so she and Guillaume stopped seeing one another   the mystery was gone. Anyway   after that   she married a German   who reminded her of her mother   and her friends were grieved   but it did not last and before long she was back to the rue de Fleurus   but with Eric Satie now.

* * *

New lovers were like jewelry to women then   and
they always wore their new lovers whenever they
went out   or took the air as they would say. Fernande disapproved of such behavior and as a result   she and Marie Laurencin   did not get on so
well together. She has the face of a goat   Fernande
would say, but not the innocence.

Anyway. In the midst of all that   there was Picasso   always totally Picasso   listening and watching and thinking Spanish thoughts. He was busily
creating the twentieth century in those days and his
mind was anywhere but at a party when he was at a
party. One night he leaned over and said quietly in my
ear   you will sit for a portrait   no.   I said by you
and he said yes. I said you betcha.

Well.

He had not worked with a model for over eight years
Picasso and then only once and so I went to his studio
to pose and there followed some ninety sittings.

Sometimes at the sittings Fernande would make tea
and Picasso would discuss his ideas especially those
concerned with cubism. You start with an object he
would say and then you strip away all the traces of
reality from it. There is nothing to fear because the
idea of the object will continue to be present and it is
the idea not the object that is important. He was talking about painting of course   but his ideas were
pertinent to my thoughts on literature at the time   to
start with an object and then strip all the traces of
reality from it   so that only the idea of the object
can be perceived   and that is what I did with some of

the characters in *Three Lives* and I have Picasso's genius to thank for it. When he was little   his mother used to tell him that if he became a soldier he would be a general and if he became a priest he would be the pope. Instead he became an artist and ended up as Picasso.

But he was a simple man   a warm one   and the sittings like the long walks across the Seine were a source of inspiration for me and we became great friends   Picasso and I   we were alike in many ways   and then one day   without any warning he suddenly dipped a cloth in turpentine and wiped my face right off the canvas. I cannot see you anymore he said and that was the end of the sittings. He went to Spain and back before he painted in the face again   and this time he did it without a model and it looked like a mask   an African one   the eyes were almond shaped and one was larger than the other. Oh, I loved it immediately   everyone else was merely astonished. But she does not look like that someone finally said. She will   he said.

Well while he was in Spain   I finished the book I was writing   but it was written in pencil and it was difficult to read and unfortunately typing is one of the things that makes me nervous   then Etta Cone took pity   Miss Etta Cone   one of my oldest friends from Baltimore   and she offered to type the manuscript for me. She and her sister   Claribel   had often come to visit me while I posed for Picasso   and he had persuaded them to buy the complete collection of his more obscure sketches   in other words the discards   which were to him nothing more than litter   but they did not know that the Cone sisters   they thought it was a valuable esoteric collection   and so they paid him something like two dollars apiece for each sketch and he was happy   Picasso because he enjoyed taking Americans for a ride   and the Cone sisters went away happy because their collection of Picassos was to become the heart of the Baltimore Museum of Art.

So anyway   Miss Etta Cone typed out the book for me and then we sent it to a friend in New York who submitted it to a publisher and it was rejected   immediately rejected. It is an enormous thing being rejected   it makes one feel funny   I did   and I automatically turned to my brother for encouragement   mistake. After he had read the book   which he did not want to do   he was silent noncommittal   painfully so. He was beginning to lose the little patience he had with people   Leo   he was beginning to be going deaf   going what   going deaf   yes it is   thank you very much.

Leo had also just given up on cubism at that time he said he could not take it seriously anymore   he said he knew its origins too well and considered them ludicrous. For all his efforts and energies put forth on behalf of modern art he was to secede from the movement at that point and to be left behind utterly by this revolution in art.

He had been the most effective   and impressive connoisseur of this art in the world   in the whole world. He had recognized Picasso and Matisse   not just one or the other as everybody else had   but that they were related in ways which they were not even aware of   Picasso and Matisse and this relation was visible only to him   Leo   and it was important to him and to the world then too   and now he was going to turn

24 his back on Matisse   not just Picasso   but Matisse
and the whole thing with cubism.

For Leo the portrait of me by Picasso was as a whole
incoherent   and that was when my conversations
with Picasso began to grow and my dialogues with
Leo began to diminish.

Picasso said   and I agreed   that at that time   ugliness and the confrontation of ugliness in art was beginning to unsettle people's pictures of life just a
bit   everyone's definition of ugliness was beginning
to grow vague and it was understandable   the nineteenth century was in a total state of inertia with re-
gards to esthetics until just toward the end   when it
began to break and give way to the explosion that
was   and is   the twentieth century. Always before   ugliness was an effrontery to traditional esthetics   but once those traditions were thrown into
question by the fact that a painting can totally dis-
regard   and in fact challenge   one's concept of
beauty   and still remain an intense and pleasurable
experience, then everyone's definition of what con-
stitutes ugly started to become vague indeed.

Well   if you make a painting of a violin and you
leave out the violin someone will inevitably call it
ugly. But if it is the absence of the violin that makes
it a painting of a violin   then something interesting
has been accomplished. A violin is just a violin unless
someone plays it or paints it   it is just a thing   but
if you play it it becomes a feeling and if you paint it
it becomes a feeling too   it ceases to be a thing
then   a painting is never the thing that it is a painting
of   it is a feeling about that thing   and so a paint-

ing of a violin without a violin in it can still be a painting of a violin and even a good one   it may not be
traditional   but it is true nonetheless   and unlike
Leo   I was not interested in principles of art   it
was his interest in them that held him back. One was
always aware with Leo's creations of his meticulously
studied techniques   there is no doubt about that   but
he always quit   always gave in before he was
through   before he achieved that feeling   because
he was afraid that in the end it would not be there and
that is generally the case with quattrocento art ex-
perts   who know so much about how a painting is
painted that they misplace   the ability to comprehend why. A child with a piece of chalk and a black-
board is a potential Sistine Chapel in a way   the
cave men did it on the walls of their caves and although it was not Rembrandt   it was art   theirs
was art   now   that is not nonsense.

Anyone can criticize   but not everyone can do   as
was the case with Mr. Leo   and if his tastes were beginning to revert back to the conservative   mine
were not   they were continuing to be moving ahead
and I was already planning another book. This was to
be my thousand-page book. I planned calling it *The
Making of Americans*   and it was to have no beginning no middle no end   just a continuous flow of
repeated words and phrases   words and phrases with
gradual variations   in other words   sheer cubism.

Picasso did not understand   he did not think it could
be done in literature   and so he asked Leo about it.
Leo was full of silent disapproval naturally   and
could not be bothered   he had just figured out the
secret of what makes a sonnet tick   and so Picasso

was left out in the dark and I had no one with whom I could discuss the headful of ideas I was carrying around with this thousand-page book   really no one.

And then the San Francisco earthquake hap-pened   which changed my life.

Lights Fade
to a
Curtain

ACT TWO

Lights slowly fade up. We discover GERTRUDE as we left her but staring concentratedly into space. A jolt of thunder shocks her into the present. She sips from the iced tea at her elbow and speaks as just having spoken.

The San Francisco earthquake   which changed my life.

Now Michael Stein and his wife Sally   were living in Paris at the time of the earthquake   Michael dear Michael   who had supported Leo and me the whole time we were in Paris   Michael was the eldest of my brothers as Leo was the youngest   Simon and Berthe were in the middle   he was simple and she had a habit of grinding her teeth at night   but to keep to the subject.

Michael and Sally frantically returned to San Francisco after the news of the disaster to survey any damages that might have been wrought on their home or the family business   and they took with them several new Matisses   which were the first of their kind in America   and that is how the new movement spread across the ocean.

San Francisco   was a total wreck when they got there   only the frame structures had withstood the earthquake because they were flexible   and so nature had provided us all with a little lesson   one must be flexible if one is to survive Michael and Sally were flexible and their house was flexible too and so was the family business fortunately and everybody then was happy. And so before they returned to Paris Michael and Sally showed their new Matisses to their neighbor   Harriet Levy   and she told her next-door neighbor about them.

Now the next-door neighbor was a real character a paradox she liked a view she said   but she liked to sit with her back to it   that was the next-door neighbor. She had plans to be a concert pianist   she had studied under a pupil of Franz Liszt   she was a real gypsy this one   but her plans were halted when her mother died and she found herself elected to the role of the responsible daughter in a houseful of cigar-smoking men   in other words   the cleaning woman.

Her father's name was Ferdinand and Ferdinands are usually always dynastic   anyway this one was   he had his father and he had his son living under the same roof as himself   daughters were of no con-sequence   and so he relegated   delegated   rele-gated . . . *(after considering the appropriateness of either word Gertrude rises and finds a dictionary through which she thumbs and searches while mum-bling)* to Alice all of the responsibilities of seeing to the domestic details   her name was Alice   it still is   and she has an amazing faculty for sleeping eter-nally on rainy days. *(she has been reading a definition and, discovering its fitness joyously cries out to the audience)* RELEGATED. *(She replaces the diction-ary on a table beside her.)*

Well anyway   Alice was living with her father in San Francisco at the time of the quake   do wake up she said   the city has been demolished. Oh really   he said   that will give us a bloody nose in the east   and went back to sleep. The Toklas family's sense of hu-mor is an unusually arid one and frequently disarm-

ing   Alice has been called frightening more than
once.

She frightened Ernest Hemingway   of all people   but
that was many years later   and in her early days in
San Francisco   she was quite a charming apparition.
She wore Chinese silks a lot and Spanish shawls and
she rode a horse. When she swept into the cafés   they
used to say   is that you Carmen   she was very
popular at the literary clubs. And then her grandfather
died   then the earthquake happened   and Alice decided it was time to escape to someplace far away and
romantic.

She mentioned the idea to her neighbor, Harriet Levy
and Harriet was very encouraging   in fact   she
offered to join her   and so they booked passage on a
ship and sailed to France. Alice flirted with the Com-
modore along the way   but it did not become seri-
ous   although he did send her a note the day after
they arrived in Paris   which she of course tore up
and threw into the lake at the Tuileries. That evening
she and Harriet called on Michael and Sally Stein   I
was there by chance   and that is when I first met
Alice Toklas   the B is for Babette.

She was immediately taken with the coral brooch I
was wearing   to her it was as if my voice emanated
from it. We had tea and then I invited Alice to come
to the rue de Fleurus the next afternoon so we could
take a walk. She arrived late by half an hour and I met
her at the door.

I said   you are late   and perhaps I did not have my
friendly voice of the day before. I paced up and down

a great deal and certain matters were made clear   very clear   very clear. Now you understand I said and we took the walk. She was never late again.

We walked in the Luxembourg gardens   it was the first of our many walks there   and I pointed out all the flowers and said   are they not lovely Alice   and she said   they certainly are Miss Stein   she was not one to take the familiar without premeditation.

It was not until the following Saturday night when she accepted an invitation to dine with us at the rue de Fleurus and the Picassos arrived late that she finally became more relaxed and called me Gertrude. Here we are late as usual   said Fernande as she glided into the dining room as if they owned the place and Picasso was saying   they were both talking at once   *je sais*   he said   I know I know punctuality is the courtesy of kings   Helene said the next time she would fry the eggs for sure and I said   a cold soufflé is a cold soufflé   and Alice called me Gertrude. Leo was still sulking   we had argued earlier in the day about Plato   and who cares   he was getting to be as bad as the Duncans.   Well before you knew it   Alice had made herself quite indispensable at twenty-seven rue de Fleurus   she was in and out a lot running errands and doing favors for every-body   and it was not long before Harriet Levy began to get in the way. It took a while to manipu-late   to arrange for her to go back to America   but not before the spinach supper at the Picassos that was to be known the world over as the famous banquet Rousseau.

Alice and I were at that time going everywhere in Paris together   we had discovered in one another a

mutual fondness for cakes   cakes of all varieties   and
so we took in all the bakeries   and we ran into Fernande in one of them   Harriet Levy was with us
naturally.   Fernande said   oh we are having a supper in honor of Rousseau   and I said   oh   who
is Rousseau   she said it did not matter   and to let
her see   yes   our names were on the list. Even
Harriet Levy's. And the supper was to be rice   not
spinach   but things do not always turn out as they
are planned as Fernande was soon to discover. And
Harriet Levy.

Well as it turned out   Rousseau was a painter and
Picasso had bought one of his portraits   a large
one   and the rice supper was to be in honor of the
new purchase. Fernande had gone to great lengths to
plan the menu and everything but the rice   Spanish
rice incidentally   was to be catered. As for Picasso
he was quite pleased with his acquisition   he found
the new works by Rousseau very exciting   Leo liked
them not   as usual. They are all right I suppose   he
said   I mean I like the native villagers in Africa
too   but I do not want them living in my home.

It began   as all things do   in the afternoon   not
that all things begin in the afternoon   but that all
things do begin and this one began in the afternoon.
Although accounts do differ. Several of the guests had
gathered earlier in the little café at the foot of the hill
the Picassos lived on   and we were all intent on having an aperitif   before going to the banquet. Well
nobody ever stops   with one.

Before long Marie Laurencin was up and dancing   drunk of course   and calling everyone by
their initials. Oh, L.S., G.A., G.S.   What is that   Alice

said pointing at Marie Laurencin. That is M.L. I said. Willowy. Said Alice.

The next to go was Harriet Levy   she got the hiccups   and just about the time we were all to make our way up that hill   Fernande entered the café and said very solemnly   stay longer I burned the rice. Well we all sat back down again   except Alice   who rose to her calling. Taking charge of the crisis   she departed with Fernande to buy more rice   then Apollinaire left to fetch the guest of honor   while the rest of us started up that hill.

Marie Laurencin did not have an easy time of it   she had the use of her legs all right   but had lost all sense of direction   so Leo and I exchanged her back and forth   until we got to the top. Fernande and Alice passed us halfway up the hill they had found rice nowhere in the Latin Quarter and so they bought spinach instead.

At the Bateau Lavoir   Picasso had elaborately enshrined the painting by Rousseau with garlands of flowers and draperies. The spinach was cooking downstairs in Max Jacob's studio and when Leo and I got there with what was left of Marie Laurencin, Fernande became abusive, really abusive   and she barred the doorway. She is not coming in here   she said   it is not that kind of a party. I said   oh   come on   we had such a terrific struggle getting her up that hill   and Fernande looked at me   but she gave in and silently returned to the kitchen to chop things.

And then someone rushed in and said that Apollinaire was coming up the hill with the guest of honor   and

Fernande put down the butcher knife   quietly sat down in a chair   and then she screamed. Because the caterers had not yet arrived with the rest of the dinner. Alice very calmly telephoned them. She is like that   but there was no answer   and Fernande said   forget it   we eat spinach. Well we all sat down   and Apollinaire ushered in Rousseau   who was a very gentle and dignified old man. That is Rousseau   said Marie Laurencin   shocked   and Apollinaire took her off to one side. This is not that kind of a party he said.

Rousseau took his seat at the place of honor   a little throne made by Picasso   and then Fernande came to the table   announced that there was enough spinach here to feed all of Paris and we clapped our hands and ate heartily and drank wine. Apollinaire recited a verse he had written for the occasion   and Marie Laurencin   who had been relatively docile for a brief spell   suddenly burst out in wild cries. Apollinaire had to take her downstairs this time and when they came back she was sober   but by then   another of the guests was up on the table with a glass of wine in one hand and throwing punches with the other   and the men carried him off and put him in the coat room where he slept peacefully and agreeably for the rest of the night. Fernande was in a far corner of the room   beating her forehead with her fists and remonstrating   while Picasso laughed   which only infuriated her more   and then the gypsies arrived with the donkey   and Fernande turned to Rousseau   and said   well it is no use trying to fool you anymore   she said   it is that kind of a party   and it was.

36   Later in the evening   when Marie Laurencin was in a better humor   she sang some old Norman songs with traditional melodies that had never been written down and as I recall there was some Spanish dancing too but that might have been another time anyway   after Alice and I declined to sing songs of the American Indians   Leo and Picasso finally persuaded Rousseau to play his violin.

Leo put on his hearing aid for the event and Rousseau performed works by Rousseau. Alice and Leo share a deep loving of the violin and both were profoundly moved by the old man's blissful gentle playing. The festivities continued until all hours   despite the ultimate departure of the guest of honor   who at one point merely leaned against the wall   slid to the floor and nodded off. As a result he missed the delirium tremens spectacle that was done so well by Crimnitz   he actually chewed a bar of soap and foamed at the mouth   which undid Alice   absolutely undid her   horrible she said.

Then one of the candles on the wall began to drip wax onto Rousseau's head and the wax accumulated and formed into a little cone   and no one dared disturb him. Well as the evening progressed   Max Jacob told Alice's fortune   and said she had a tendency towards theft   and Alice looked at me   and then we conferred and then Alice asked Max if he saw any travel in the immediate future for Harriet Levy   and he said no   and I fixed on his eyes and said   try harder. Oh I understand he said. In a few minutes he drew Harriet over to one side and began describing a psychic revelation concerning her that had just swept over him. And then the donkey got into the coat room

where it proceeded to eat a telegram   a box of
matches   and the feathers on Alice Toklas's hat.
Alice was not amused.

At about three in the morning we all finally gave
out. Leo and I put Alice and Harriet and the gentle
Rousseau into a cab and took them home. The next
day   Fernande and Picasso were awakened by a
knock at the door. It was the caterers of course and
they had finally arrived with the dinner. Now you
might think that that was the end of the banquet Rousseau but it was not long after that that Harriet Levy
took the advice of her new astrologer   Max Jacob   packed her things to return to America   and
that was the end of Harriet Levy.

Well here's to good ole Rousseau and everybody's
inner life   which brings me to the subject of why I
left America and came to Paris   which has a lot to
do with everything   especially identity   identity.

Identity is an interesting thing   what happens to
identity and memory when they are confronted with
eternity   eternity   that has always worried me.
My mother was very nice and very dull   whatever
my father said was what she thought. She provided
us with everything we needed except an interesting
mother and then she died. And we all said   well. Our
father now was what one would call an authoritarian
and when he died we were all rather relieved   especially Leo.

After the funerals   when Leo went to Harvard   I got
passed around the family for a while. They finally decided to send me to college   college   college   col-

lege. If she is marriageable it will happen to her there and if she is not she will be able to get herself one of the better jobs and support herself.

Well I loathe that word job loathe the whole concept to me it meant imprisonment and my inner life was threatened. But I went to college anyway Harvard well Radcliffe but it was Harvard and studied psychology with Dr. William James alongside my brother Leo. I made it to my final year at medical school Johns Hopkins University and would have been oh yes a doctor had I never met May Bookstaver there. May had a certain quality that reminded me of the girls at Radcliffe and since none of those Radcliffe girls ever liked me and she did we became very close intimate. Americans like things to be all alike it is an art with them if not an obsession and anything that is different is a. Curiosity to them. I was going to say threat. Well in America with everything so standardized lives people relationships it is difficult to be noticeably different and I was.

I was fat very fat very fat.

It is an interesting thing being fat being fat is a state of mind it keeps you from having to fulfill certain frightening expectations and gives you a chance to live in your own little world. Once May had lured me out of mine I was grateful to her for her friendship and I came to depend on her as I did Leo for everything. It was inconceivable to me at the time why she that pretty little thing and almost bright too would have dropped me for a companion who was merely less vulnerable and more sophisticated.

Well May Bookstaver   FAT   Being different   People politely averting their eyes   May
Bookstaver   Jobs   Identity   Senility and grandchil-
dren and how to avoid them   both   Jobs   May
Bookstaver   Mother and father and how they would
have loved to dance at my wedding   May Bookstaver
and Eternity   Good night Dr. Stein   Good night
Dr. Bookstaver Not possible. Certainly I left America.
Period.

Years later when Alice found the letters May had
written me   she burned them. In a passion she said.
Well Alice is like that and sometimes her passions are
a treat and that is very lovely.

With Harriet gone   Alice Toklas was free at last to
accept my invitation to move into twenty-seven rue
de Fleurus and to become a member of the household.
The year was nineteen hundred and nine and Leo
was very accommodating about the whole thing. He
even gave up his study for Alice to use as her bed-
room   sometimes I think he thought her presence at
the *pavillon* would take the burden of producing enthusiasm for my writing off his shoulders   and perhaps after all it did   for Alice was very enthusias-
tic   and she also had a flair for typing   quite a
flair.

Alice was astounded   she was astonished   that my
first book had met with rejection even once much less
a half-dozen times   so she said   print it yourself   goose. Well of course. So *Three Lives* was sent
off to the Grafton Press in New York   who special-
ized in limited editions that were of course paid for
out of the author's pocket.

40 They were a little worried   the publishers   about my punctuation   which they did not consider satisfactory   and they sent a courier to Paris to discuss with me the matter of proofreading. But it is proofread I said   What about the question marks he said   there are no question marks. I said   question marks are out of the question. Anybody with any sense knows a question when he sees one and does not need any little marks to tie his shoes for him. Well surely you will want to put in a few more commas he said   he kept looking at me and then quickly looking at Alice   and then back at me again. I said   it is true   she is watching you very closely   and after he left   Alice counted the silverware   she was not fond of publishers   no.

Anyway   he was not about to leave until I agreed to put in at least one more comma   and I said   put in another comma   are you out of your mind   period. We followed him to the courtyard laughing and shouting about apostrophic contractions and the evils thereof.

By the fall of nineteen eleven   I had finished my book   my second one   a thousand pages long   Alice typed every one of them herself   and it was long. It was no longer the history of a family   but had somehow become a history of everybody   well there were so many pages to fill.

For Leo   *The Making of Americans* was about nine hundred and ninety-nine pages too long. Leo was so much more adventuresome when we were younger. How did he get to be so staid.

I was always the shy one but as we got older it is

odd how our roles seemed almost to reverse   I was
no longer following and he was no longer lead-
ing   very strange   very   and analysis is what did
it to him. He was never successful at shaping his character around his limitations once he had identified
them   he could not accept his limitations   much
less learn to love them   and that is a very important
key to being an artist.

It is a funny thing creating   a book is you make
it   and you make it for yourself and for stran-
gers   and you make it by working hard   and it becomes your life then and then one day you are finished
and you want to show it to everyone and you are
afraid to show it to anyone   and someone looks at it
and reads it; and you wonder if they will say yes or
no   yes is what you want   of course   it is always very pleasant   yes   but no is what every
writer   every artist is afraid of.

As for Alice she had gathered up and typed every day
what I had written down the night before   and
later we would have tea and read through the pages
together   always quite surprised by what we
found   because it was all done rather spontane-
ously   as time passed we took to referring to it as the
daily miracle. It was quite a ritual with us. Alice. Alice
was my yes and that was very important.

Even a no can be a yes if it is done right. For example.
Alice and I mailed off the manuscript of *The Making
of Americans* to a Mr. Fifield   a publisher in Eng-
land and he responded by sending back my manuscript
along with a letter that said   Dear Madam   there
will be others will be others will be others other
styles   other books   other publishers thank you;

thank you   no thank you no thank you no. And although it was a rejection it was not a no no no   it was a yes   an unmistakable one   and that is what critics refer to as style; style.

So we decided Alice and I   to go off to Spain together   to celebrate Mr. Fifield's stylish rejection of my novel   and we created a sensation in the villages with our clothes. Alice always carried her fan and wore black   my Spanish disguise   she said. I wore my robe and sandals   the villagers followed me everywhere   they thought I was a bishop.

It is interesting   I discovered while we were there in Spain that I have a faculty for creating new languages when the ones that are present do not do; and in Spain English and French do not do   and so not knowing any Spanish   I had to improvise   and they always understood me   the villagers   at least they looked like they did   and I was able to experiment with the sounds of words instead of their definitions   with textures rather than meanings   and I came up with some incredible new combinations   and so Spain proved to be for me   as it was for Picasso   a place of inspiration.

With this new form   and it was totally disarming   it really was   I created word portraits of people I know. I did Matisse   and I did Picasso   but the first of them was Alice. I called it Ada   but it was Alice   and I showed it to her   baffling   said Alice   wonderful I said   and then we went to Italy to Mabel Dodge's villa just outside Florence   and that was where it happened. My brother made me angry. An opera.

We spent the autumn there together   Leo joined
us   and I wrote the portrait of Mabel Dodge
at the Villa Curonia in my newly discovered
style   which Mabel had published at her own ex-
pense and bound in florentine wallpaper   Leo was
incensed.

He thought my portrait of Mabel was not only obscure   but a hoax   an elaborate hoax   and I was
furious   but then he wrote a sarcastic parody of Mabel's portrait and I pretended to understand it   and
that made him even angrier until finally he confided
in Mabel that he thought I was growing foolish and
helpless in his opinion because of Alice   he said she
did everything to save me a step   and it was a clear
case of the weaker enslaving the stronger   he had
seen trees choked to death by vines in the same fash-
ion   yes the noun was vines and the verb was choked.

When Mabel told me that I laughed   and said
that that is exactly how I feel about the use of commas   but inside it made me feel funny that he saw
Alice in that light   it made me feel funny   and
Alice sensed it too. Well by the end of the autumn
when we returned to the rue de Fleurus   everything
came out into the open.

To begin with   Leo stopped associating himself with
the Saturday evenings altogether   he said he was no
longer able to endure talking art to just anyone who
happened in   he said he would rather cope with
demons.

One night after everybody was gone   or gone to
bed   I want to talk to you   he said. Well   I
said. And that was the beginning of act four. Ger-

trude   he said. Cubism is tommyrot. Whether it is done with a paint brush or a fountain pen   it is tommyrot   tommyrot   tommyrot   tommyrot.

Tommyrot.

Well I had to sit down after that.

And as for Picasso's latest works he continued   they are for my money utterly obnoxious   somebody asked me the other day if I do not think them quite mad   I said   pitifully no   they are not that in-triguing at all   just stupid.

He said that   he actually said   that   and then he accused me   I suppose he wanted me to confess. Gertrude   said he   you obviously have no interest in the criticism of ideas   go on I said   he said   that is a strong indication that your main interests lie in the pursuit of glory   and I said   hold it   right there.

He said   it is true   you have always desired glory from life   even as far back as nineteen ought ought   you were verbose about it   walking along the Grand Canal   you kept saying it over and over   glory   *la gloire*   *la gloire*   I said   so what   he said   Gertrude   that is vain.

I said   all right   vain so.

He said   Gertrude there is no room in art for vanity. And I said   wait a minute quattrocento art expert. He looked at me like I had stabbed him   and then I said   what about Leonardo   what about Michel-angelo   what about Titian with his thing for red hair   are you telling me those boys were above vanity.

He looked at me but he said nothing.

I said   Leo glory   *la gloire* is very pretty   yes but
it is just a mere tool   he said this ought to prove interesting   and I said   in order to gain a foot-
hold   gather a following   you have to do the
things that you have to do that get you an audience   and then once you have them   lis-
teners   readers   spectators   you become responsible   you have to   because they are your children
then and that is a responsibility   you are obliged to
them   they care about what you think in order to
dare to think new thoughts of their own   and he
said   the responsibility   little mother   ought to
come first not after. And then I was speechless.
Well his eyes positively dilated at that point and he
said   sort of smiling   let me dichotomize *la gloire*
for you   and then my eyes dilated and suddenly I
was not speechless   anymore   and I said oh by all
means do.

He said   in two words   I like the term publish   Gertrude   for me it holds a certain dig-
nity   and you like the term publicity   I said what
difference really   they both have that pub   I mean
they both have that pub. He said   oh hell you give
me nonsense   and I said   if that is nonsense then I
am someone else   someone else   someone else   and
he always hated when I did that.

Well dust settles.

I said   finally it is not a matter of responsibility and
timing then   finally it is a matter of some people
feeling that they are expected by the world to share

what they think by the whole world and some people feeling that the world ought to expect them to share what they think. He said is that the way you think it is with you and me and I said what do you think.

Then he said.

Gertrude   remember when you were a little girl   and I knew it was going to be long then   and I said   yes   and he said   remember going to school and how you were obliged to enter an art contest   and I remembered   I remembered   because ever since I have considered competition to be not interesting.

Well competition   just allowing it to occur naturally is one thing   but in America from kindergarten all the way up to the first heart attack they encourage it   with a special emphasis on winning   they do love their competitive sports   especially the arena   the actual arena   the stadium. You would think the Italians would be the ones   being descended from the Romans   but no   the only ones who love the arena more than the Americans are the Spaniards. Germans love the bullfights too   but as Pablo always said   with Spaniards   it is the ritual and with Germans it is the bloodshed. What got me off on this   oh my brother Leo's telling me about when I was a little girl in school.

I said   what has that got to do with anything Leo   and he said   oh let me show you   he said remember when you got home that day from school and your brothers all sat down and tried to explain to you how to take a cup and saucer in front of you and outline it on paper and you   were incapable   to-

tally   of grasping that   totally   just froze your
mind   and I said yes   and he said   that carried
on into medical school did it not   you were unable
to draw anatomical studies   because you could not
for the life of you figure out how one goes about
taking a real shape and depicting its concavities or
convexities on paper. And I said   yes   and he
said   you never really learned how to draw a para-
graph either   did you   how to construct one and
I said no I have these limitations.

Well he said   who finally took and drew the cup
and saucer for you which you then took with you
back to school and won the prize. I said you did Leo.

He said   that is just about what you did with
art   Gertrude   with cubism   I did it all for you
he said and then you went out and won the prize. And
lost it. While playing in a field on the way home from
school and that he said   is very Freudian   and I
said   you are very Freudian. He said he felt cheated
somehow and I said oh. Identity is a funny thing when
threatened   it is funny that we both should have
ended up as threats to one another's inner lives by
our very existence. I do not know why it was that
way   but it was   and he knew that it was. Well it
just was.

And then he said   you and Picasso have both gone
off into your respective so-called abstract tan-
gents   and nobody can understand what you are
doing or trying to do. Your artistic abilities are I
think   extremely limited. And then he attacked my
book my thousand-page book   he said   my mind
was as little nimble as a mind could be   and that my

attempts to emulate Picasso's latest form in my writing were not just affected but pathetically comical.

I rose and said   is that all   he said no   and I sat back down.

He said he had talked to Picasso recently about art he said   and that Picasso had finally come to the realization   that although   art should be instinctive   it should be filtered through and developed by the intellect of the artist. He liked to use your favorite idols   Leo   when he was setting you up for something. He said   you and Picasso are both using a pair of intellects that you ain't got to do what requires the very sharpest critical aplomb   which you ain't got neither   to turn out not just mediocre stuff   but the most godalmighty trash imaginable. He said   better to produce nothing my dear   than to produce garbage. Well   I left the room then   and decided before I went to sleep that it was quite obviously   time for brother and sister to part.

The dividing up of the great Stein collection was a shock to everyone   but it was done pleasantly. Leo took his portion of the Renaissance furniture and the Cézanne apples   and Picasso painted this apple for Alice and me to take its place   and the rest we just sort of divided up equally.

By spring   Leo was settled in his new home and he wrote from Florence and said that we should all live happily ever after sucking contentedly on our separate oranges.

We had been companions for a long time   he and I   he had been my friend for forty years. Little by

little we never saw each other   or wrote   or spoke
after that.

It is a funny thing   this genius thing. Why me and
not him. Why not him. Why not him instead of
me. Instead of me instead of him. Why me and not
him. Sometimes when I think about it   it makes me
feel   well anyway.

After that   it really was just Alice and myself alone
together at the *pavillon*   rather peaceful   and we
still held receptions on Saturday nights. Alice fixed
things for everyone to eat   she is always good at
that   nobody ever turned down anything she
made   except that fudge. Well by and by   Carl
Van Vechten   began dropping by   we had met
him at the theatre   and we became great friends.
In rapid time   we became almost a middle-class
family   Carl was Papa Woojums   Alice was Mama
Woojums   and as for Baby Woojums   well I do
not want to think about that now.

And then the Germans invaded Belgium and war was
declared. War. In my lifetime. Just because the politicians in one country were mad at the politicians in
another country   politicians can be damned uninteresting at times   but it is not their fault entirely as the ordinary people always seem to be needing a dictator   whether he is a nice one or a mean
one   they do   they always seem to be needing one.
Really   really   there are too many excellencies-in-
chief running around on this planet. People can take
care of themselves   they do not need all these daddies. Daddies are like commas. Period.   Oh war is
such an uninteresting thing   it really is   as long as
people just blindly   just blindly   allow themselves

to be used by their politicians as resources towards political ends   well then   they can never look upon
wars as anything other than something that just
happens   just happens   destiny   and so naturally   they develop about as much insight into wars
as mice do into lab experiments.

In wartime   everybody is always talking about
freedom and liberty   well not everybody   some
people are talking about how impossible it is to get
butter   real butter   but most people are   and
the trouble is   anyone who equates political liberty   which is local   with freedom   which is abstract is not thinking period.

Well anyway   as long   as there was going to be a
war   Alice and I decided that we must do our share
to make it a less destructive one   and we offered
our services to the American Fund for the French
Wounded. They needed people desperately to deliver
emergency supplies all over the country and they
asked us if we drove a truck. Alice and I looked at each
other. The next thing we knew   Alice and I were
driving a truck   that is   I was driving   Alice
was in the passenger seat saying   no no   over
there   be careful   oh dear   a lot. I drove everywhere   except in reverse   I could never master
going backwards   in circles   yes   but not backwards   that is the road to becoming a quattrocento
art expert. Pretty soon we were driving all over
France   through mud and snow and flat tires   nobody ever told me about flat tires   we got a lot of
flat tires and we picked up hitchhikers   soldiers. Nobody knows how to patch a flat like a hitchhiking
American soldier.

American soldiers became a regular feature at tea time at the rue de Fleurus   Alice and I enjoyed talking to them very much   the thing they liked most about Alice and me was that we listened. We still hear from one or two of them now and then. Wars make it impossible to live on an income   nobody can   anyway   I sold the painting of the lady with the hat   and when I asked Alice what we were having for dinner that night she said   The Matisse   of course.

Still it was a hard winter   especially for Alice with the zeppelin raids at night   but some nights we were able to go for walks. The night that Apollinaire was dead   Picasso and I took a walk together   and along the way we encountered a parade of cannons   big ones   big   big ones   that were going down his street. It was the first time any of us had seen anything that was painted in camouflage   and it looked like cubism   the painting on the cannons   and Picasso wept   and said a little prayer   We have created this   he said   and look what it has come to   and I wept with him then   while the cannons disappeared into the dark at the end of the street   the long dark at the end of the street. The day peace was declared Alice was the one who told me   I could breathe again   the shadow had passed but it had left its mark.

After the war   a lot of American writers were coming to Paris to meet me   some of them expatriates like myself   America was still my country   but Paris was my home town   and these writers were all looking for something and I had it   and they knew it   and they wanted it too. They wanted to meet me   and they gathered at Sylvia Beach's book shop   each one of them imploring her to give them introduction to me.

Well Sylvia could never say no to Scott Fitzgerald and so we got to meet Scotty and his wife   he made the mistake of bringing his wife to twenty-seven rue de Fleurus.

Wives bother me   they bore me   oh they bore me stiff. They could not be actually prevented from com-ing but once there   they were snatched aside and kept out of the way by Alice   who was under strict orders to keep them occupied with their favorite con-versation topics which usually boiled down to hats and you are never going to believe what I paid for these shoes and things like that. Alice was very good at it. Frighteningly so. She was such a little cat   Alice   but her favorite mouse was Hemingway's wife.

Now the Hemingways   were too happily married to be believed   her name was Hadley   they came in-troduced by Sherwood Anderson   and goodness they were young   he was twenty-three   Ernest   and they were both a little afraid of Alice. She was doing her needlepoint when they arrived and she smiled and continued her needlework and she saw to the refresh-ments and saw to Hadley   and listened to Ernest and me   and everytime Hadley leaned forward a little too far in her seat   Alice would pass her more hot tea.

Well Hemingway was a mass of fears and preju-dices   he said he had always carried a knife when he traveled in the company of men   because in those

days   when he was a boy   there were a lot of
wolves about   and wolves was not a term for men
who chased after women at that time. He said if a man
sensed that you would kill then you were let be and
not interfered with in certain ways   Alice de-
tested him forever after that. But I was patient with
him   well   he was so young and his eyes were so
passionately interested and he was sitting at my feet
as though I was the goddess of intelligence   so I
proceeded to instruct him on the subject of sex. You
are really very ignorant about all of this   Hemingway   I said   but you have a right to your dis-
gust   because with men it is an ugly thing   whereas
with women it is beautiful   that is why men who are
that way take to drink and use drugs and are never
really happy changing partners all the time. I see he
said. But with women it is exactly the opposite and
that is why you hardly ever hear about it. I see   he
said.

Well he took everything so seriously   except the
shallowness of his young mind   and he did not know
when he was being made sport of but it was good for
him   he needed it. Some time later   after it all sank
in he sent me a very brief note that said   a bitch is a
bitch   is a bitch   and it was signed your pal   and
I was glad then because it meant he understood and
nothing more needed to be said. Well   he was a good
fellow when he was young I thought and some of his
really early stuff was not so bad   but he never got
along with Alice and so our friendship did not last   it
faded   but not the flowers of it   never the flowers.

Another friendship that faded fast was my friendship
with Sylvia Beach. She actually   Sylvia actually published a signed limited edition of James Joyce's *Ulysses*.

Joyce was a name that was never mentioned at the rue de Fleurus. He was a traitor that boy   he was more involved in sensationalism than Hemingway. He had that magnificent beautiful stream of consciousness right at his fingertips and he opted for clarity. He should have stuck with those limericks. But Sylvia published him   and hardbound at that so Alice and I transferred our patronage to another book store on the Right Bank. When Sylvia confronted me and asked my why   I told her   and she said I was beginning to sound an awful lot like that brother of mine I had told her about. Well that was not to be taken lightly   I gave it a great deal of thought and then in a rather mournful gesture went home and cut off all my hair   well not really all of it   but most of it and so gradually I did not think about Sylvia's remark anymore   I lost interest   and became involved in writing a best seller   my first one.

I had often asked Alice before why she did not write an autobiography   she had surely led a fascinating life   and she could call it *My Twenty-Five Years with a Genius* or something. And she said   on top of everything else I do you want me to write books as well   do not be a goose.

So I wrote it myself her autobiography   Alice's *The Autobiography of Alice B. Toklas* by Gertrude Stein   and it became very popular   very fast   especially in America   but in Paris a group was formed to protest the publication   charging me with a list of heavy discrepancies and accusing me of indiscretions   you would have thought I had told on them or something. There was even a rumble from Italy   the land of quattrocento art   Leo was obviously wounded

because I had not made him one of the characters   nor
was he even called by name in the book   he was
simply referred to as Gertrude Stein's brother. Justice
is a dessert best served with a slight chill to it.

Nothing could have infuriated him more than knowing that a book I had written in six weeks' time had
suddenly made me a famous celebrity in Europe and
America   yes famous. Becoming a celebrity is very interesting   at least it was until the writing stopped   my
writing stopped. I did not know what to do   I
could not tell anyone   not even Alice   but when
it stopped   it stopped   and I knew it immediately inside. Money and art and identity in that
combination   in that combination are a terrific
bother   money   art and identity   they are   and
keeping them apart from one another is a piece of
intellectual juggling that no two artists can ever hope
to accomplish in the same way   and I fretted   and
Alice sensed it   but she did not know what to
do   only Woojums   Papa Woojums   could
tell   Carl   he knew   and he said   Woojums Baby
Woojums it is time   for what   for you to confront
your lionhood   really do you think so   yes.

The great American lecture tour at all the universities
in nineteen thirty-four when I was fifty-eight years
old and had just begun my lionhood by Gertrude   Gertrude Stein.

Auditoriums   Trains   Planes   Lecture Halls   Whispers   Someone coughs   and Silence. America was
amazing   it had grown so   and they were everywhere glad to see me   Carl even got me   with a
little help from Alice   on an airplane and we flew   in

the air   we actually flew in the air   what a miracle
that is   it makes the ground below look like cubism   and my writing stopped. We flew to Chicago
and there we attended an all black performance of an
opera of mine that Virgil Thomson wrote the music
for *Four Saints in Three Acts*   and my writing
stopped.

Well after the last lecture   before we went back
home   Alice and I were invited to New York to
meet the Mr. Bennett Cerf of the Random House
publishing company   which was the most telling
of all our experiences there   and my writing
stopped   Americans are so funny about clothing   and
when Alice and I showed up at Random House   they
took one look at us and immediately sent us to the
personnel supervisor in charge of maintenance   Alice
was absolutely devastated   indeed she said   and my
writing stopped.

But we finally got upstairs to talk with Bennett
Cerf   and we talked about everything from cubism
to mystery stories   I told him about my predilection
for mystery stories   I could read a mystery story
a day for the rest of my life   I love mystery
stories   everything is a mystery story   sitting   doing
nothing   thinking is a mystery story   will she ever
go and wake up Alice or will Alice have to sleep forever   everything is   and I love mystery stories   and
so he said   Bennett Cerf said   if you love mystery
stories so much   why do you not write them   and
I said   but I do   write them   the beginnings and
the endings are always quite obvious   but nobody
can ever guess the middles. Oh he said   and then he
said he would publish a book of mine a year for the
next four years. Alice was ecstatic   but inside I was

thinking   oh wonderful now that the writing has
stopped. And then we left for home.

Whom did we first bump into when we got there but
Fernande Olivier and Marie Laurencin   and that was
the beginning of the final act.

Fernande was in a fit   and Marie Laurencin was
just sort of green colored   what is it   I said   horrible said Fernande   and then she wept   and so
Marie Laurencin explained then. She said Picasso had
taken up with a bunch of surrealists who were pres-
ently in vogue   yes   yes   I said   he likes to be
voguish   and she said he had abandoned his wife
Olga   well he has done that sort of thing before I
said   remember Fernande when he left you for the
new mistress Eve   and moved from the Bateau
Lavoir   oh he's done that sort of thing before I
said   but said she   he has given up painting and
taken to writing poetry   wait a minute I said   poetry
is mine.

Well it was true   painting was his and writing was
mine   poetry was mine   and it was not funny at
all. Alice and I decided to look into the matter further   and so we paid a little visit to Picasso and I
brought along my eyeglasses so I could read some of
his stuff. Oh dear.

I love Pablo   he will always be my friend   but he
has never felt a single thing in words in his life   words
are not words are definitely not his métier.   Well I
had to say something so I took a deep breath and
said   lovely handwriting. And Alice said something
about how interesting the difference between the
Spanish and the French languages   and he knew

then   and so I said   well   let us discuss painting   and he said   let us not   I am a man of letters
now   I do not paint   I go to cafés. Well then.

We did not see each other for a while   and he continued with his writing   and then he called one day
and asked if he could bring a friend to dinner   who
is the friend said Alice   Salvador Dali said he   and
she said   well I suppose so. Well with Picasso and
dinner you can never tell and as I sort of suspected
would happen   the Dalis showed up and he did not.
He had sent them to find out what I really thought.

Salvador had written a poem too about Picasso   and
he said Picasso's poetry had made him understand his
Picasso's painting even more   and I said   oh
really   and then I took him apart one piece at a
time and deposited him on the doorstep.

Some time later   Picasso saw me on the street and
beckoned to me. Why could you tell Dali and not me
he said   because Dali is Dali and you are sensible   I
said. Dali needs to know and you already do   what
do I know he said   that you are not a poet I said   and
he said   suppose I do.   Well I shook him by the
lapels   really shook him   sometimes you have to
bully people   you just do   and I did   I shook
him hard and said   so stop trying to get me to tell
you that you are something you are not   and he
said   what am I then   and I said you are the Picasso   the phoenix of the twentieth century   and
what will I do   said he   you will paint beautiful
pictures and I will do the writing   said I   and then
I kissed him and then his face turned red and he smiled
and said   oh Zhertrude   you know me   and I
said yes   and he kissed me   and inside Vollard's   Fer-

nande Olivier and Marie Laurencin were watching and laughing and crying and hugging each other.

Well I started to write again   yes I started to write again   this time it was everybody's autobiography absolutely everybody's. We were all much older by then and in many ways we had all changed   the world had changed   only Leo had stayed the same. And Leo. The day I mailed the manuscript to Random House I saw him on the street   we did not speak   we merely nodded   and I went home then and wrote a strange thing called *How She Bowed to Her Brother*   and he went home and wrote me a letter. I received it yesterday.

I do not know if I will write him back. There are moments when I think I should. As good Professor James used to say in his lectures at Harvard those marvelous ones   always keep a little window open in the attic. Always. Not cracked. Open.

Which brings me back to something I was thinking about earlier   I thought I had lost it for sure. What happens to identity and memory when they are confronted with eternity.

I remember my first comet   seeing my first real one when I was young   and how it both thrilled and frightened me. Because it made me realize that there were big things going on out there and suddenly my little identity and my little memory seemed pretty little   and it made me wonder. I never speculate on answers though   you would have no way of knowing if you came up with the right ones   anyway   who would tell you. No the thing that is most important is coming up with the questions   the questions. It just is.

Well anyway   I was very depressed thinking about all this   and then this morning Alice woke up depressed   too   she had had a dream. What if you are the first to go   she said   Gertrude what will I do alone   and I said   there are no answers   no answers   only questions. Alice said she had been considering converting to Roman Catholicism and I said wait until I am dead to do it. And then the landlord came and his son is moving in tomorrow and then he left and it started to rain and Alice went back to bed   oh dear the sun is out   it must have stopped raining some time ago   Alice is going to kill me   nothing has been packed   I must go get her up now.   Woojums   Mama Woojums.

Still it does not seem right or possible to decimate these walls   this has been our home   it is not just an address   it is like an entity   we made this place into an international shrine of modern art   we moved out the old century and moved in another from these rooms. Well then. For people like that it should not be so difficult   memorizing   a new address. Woojums. Mama Woojums.

There. Now that I have said goodbye to this old place   I do not suppose it would hurt to send a little note to Italy informing Leo to mail all further correspondence   if any   to number five   number five what. Ah yes   number five rue Christine   this will get him   number five   rue Christine Christine Christine . . .   *And she is laughing and writing away joyously as   The lights are fading   Finally   Fading   Finally Fading*

About the Author

MARTY MARTIN, a native Texan, began his career as a dramatist at the age of ten and has since written over forty plays, a number of which received critically acclaimed productions by various theater groups throughout Texas prior to his New York debut as the author of GERTRUDE STEIN GERTRUDE STEIN GERTRUDE STEIN. Several of Mr. Martin's works are extensively researched biographical dramas, concerning such figures as Leonardo da Vinci, Sarah Bernhardt, and Sergei Diaghilev, whose lives and works were considered revolutionary for their times. As part of his preparation for the writing of his play about Gertrude Stein, Mr. Martin had his house redecorated to approximate the Stein salon, maintained the legendary Stein writing schedule and spent his mornings listening to the recordings of Gertrude Stein reading from her works. Much of his research was conducted at the University of Texas Humanities Research Center where he was able to draw from a wealth of unpublished letters and documents. Mr. Martin resides in Austin, Texas, where he devotes himself exclusively to writing for the stage.

About Pat Carroll

Louisiana-born PAT CARROLL has worked in theater, television, supper clubs, films and radio consistently for thirty-three years. She has been honored with an Emmy from the Academy of Television Arts and Sciences; an honorary Doctor of Letters degree from Barry College, Florida; and with numerous recognitions and awards for her work as Gertrude Stein (among them the Drama Desk Award as best actress for 1980). A special joy to her has been to introduce Marty Martin to professional theater by commissioning him to write GERTRUDE STEIN GERTRUDE STEIN GERTRUDE STEIN.